## About the Author

A paramedic with over twenty-five years in the ambulance service. Seen some horrific things. And some things that are just horrifically funny! Friends often say to me, how do you work with the public? You don't like people! Well, I don't mind the unconscious ones! But whether I like them or not I'll always do my best for them. And if I can get a little smile out of someone having a really bad time, then that can't be bad can it? Remember it could always be worse! Well, OK, maybe not always!

# Not at the Dinner Table

# Richard Greek

# Not at the Dinner Table

Olympia Publishers
*London*

**www.olympiapublishers.com**
OLYMPIA PAPERBACK EDITION

A CIP catalogue record for this title is
available from the British Library.

ISBN: 978-1-80439-710-7

This book is memoir. It reflects the author's present recollections of
experiences over time. Some names and characteristics have been
changed, some events have been compressed, and some dialogue
has been recreated.

First Published in 2024

Olympia Publishers
Tallis House
2 Tallis Street
London
EC4Y 0AB

Printed in Great Britain

# Dedication

I dedicated this book to my Suze and the kids Teagan, Lincoln, Alex and Amber. Thanks for all being awesome! And also, to my brothers in the yog guild – don't ask – who make me smile whatever the world throws at me!

# Acknowledgements

Thanks to the amazing people I've worked with over the years! I've worked with some truly amazing people, and I'm fairly sure you will recognise yourselves in here! To the bad ones, hopefully you recognise yourselves too! I'd also like to thank some of the amazing managers I've been lucky enough to work for. Unfortunately, you are in the minority now.

# Prologue.

Another busy Friday night in Brighton and we'd been non-stop. But we finally managed to get back to base for ten minutes. Straight away I could feel my eyelids getting heavy and I was about to doze. Suddenly the ear-shattering siren went off in the room combined with the radio on my hip beeping and vibrating to let me know we had another emergency call to attend. We both got up and went straight down to the ambulance.

It was my turn to drive so I jumped in, pushed the button to stop the noise, started the engine and then properly looked at the terrafix, our on-board computer that tells us where we are needed and why. I instantly started laughing in relief that it wasn't my turn to attend. Anne jumped in the passenger seat, took one look at my face, 'What?'

'Twenty-year-old male with a dildo stuck up his rectum!' I said.

'Oh, you're joking! Do you fancy attending this one?'

'Nope!'

And so continued another busy night, saving lives in the ambulance service!

Some people dream of becoming a paramedic. They do all the first aid they can at school. They join St John's and help out at big events. Actually, come to think of it, they also help out at small events like school fetes or open days. I'm sure some of them would turn up to the opening of an envelope if asked. But anyway, it's their dream to join the ambulance service and they work hard to achieve that dream until they finally get to pull on the greens of whichever local service they decide is right for them. It was blues when I joined but that makes me feel really old! A fact that I'm sure will be mentioned again at some point!

The thing is, I was never one of those! I had no dreams of joining the ambulance service and it was so far off my radar I barely knew it existed. I mean, obviously I knew there were ambulances, but I guess I just thought the people who worked on them were just kind of made, or magically appeared trained and ready. I didn't know what I wanted to do when I left school. It probably would have helped if I'd gone now and then, but it just didn't interest me.

When we got the chance of doing work experience at school I asked to work with cars. Like all boys of my age I had the Lamborghini and Ferrari posters on the wall and would have loved to have spent my days around them. That's how I came to be doing work experience in a Mazda garage in a pair of grotty overalls and servicing a Mazda 121! I've gotta be honest, it's not how I expected things to pan out! But I obviously did enough to impress and they offered me a job when I finished school.

Fast forward a couple of years and that hadn't really worked out for me. I'd worked there for a couple of years and liked the people, but I wasn't cut out to be a mechanic. There were just too many bits involved! Over the next six or seven years I did various jobs including a very brief stint in the RAF; they make you get up early and people keep telling you what to do! Why had no one told me that before!. And eventually found myself working in an engineering factory on night shifts. In my own way I kind of enjoyed it. The owner was a cockney geezer who said things how they were and enjoyed taking the piss out of everyone at every opportunity in between shouting or swearing at them. But I think I got on pretty well with Chris!

So, during a shift one night I walked down to the supervisor's office to see one of the supervisors in there on a computer and another guy sitting in the corner with an oily rag wrapped round his hand and looking white as a sheet! Compassionate as always. I looked at the supervisor.

'What's up with him?'

'He's just ripped his finger off in the machine.'

'Off?'

'Yep! Steve's just gone to get his car, he's gonna take him to the hospital.'

'Have you got his finger?'

'Fuck off that's gross!'

'Well, do you not think they might need it? I mean, it's his finger! It's gonna be much easier to stick back on if it isn't in a different postcode!'

This is how I came to be walking through a factory unit with a squishy bit of finger in the remains of a blue nitrile glove with a crowd of gawkers behind me.

It hadn't bothered me getting the finger out of the machine, as long as someone who knew what they were doing turned it off first. And I hadn't been thinking from a medical viewpoint. It just kind of made common sense to me that to at least try to help him they needed to have all of his bits! I bloody hate getting to the end of a puzzle to find bits are missing!

About a week after this I heard that, after the factory's summer holiday they were changing all of our shifts. They didn't sound good and I decided that I needed to get out. A few days later I had a chance meeting with an old friend of mine. We had a quick chat and asked if we'd seen any of the old crowd and then I mentioned I hadn't seen him working in the bank recently. He told me that was because he had left and was now in the ambulance service as an emergency technician. He loved it and said it was great helping people, although it helped not being squeamish. A new idea was born that would shape the next twenty years of my life.

The early years of my ambulance life were spent in the patient transport service. This is where you basically take patients for routine appointments such as fracture clinics for people unable to get there under their own steam, or for regular patients with ongoing conditions, such as renal patients, or patients who were disabled, by whatever means, to day centres.

This, in my opinion, is where you learn to talk to people, to empathise with others, to understand the basics of what the job is about. It's also where you learn to hold your breath for thirty minutes at a time, to pretend you didn't say what you definitely just said and to laugh hysterically whilst trying to hide it.

A couple of classics that many ambulance staff will recognise.
'Lift ya FEET a second, mate!' To the single amputee!
'I'll just nip outside to message control while you get ready.' At a house that smells so bad it makes your throat burn.
'Thanks for the offer but we've literally just had a cuppa!'

At a house where the cups or anything else clearly haven't been washed since 1987 despite the fact your throat is so dry you are producing dust rather than steam in the cold weather!

There was also the elderly lady who was absolutely lovely but had the most obvious wig on! Every time we leant over her to put her seatbelt on we would accidentally knock her wig sideways or backwards! We would then spend the rest of the journey trying our hardest not to laugh whilst trying to discreetly turn it the right way round before arriving at her day centre!

A sunny afternoon as a trainee tech, and Anne and I are called to a confirmed dead patient. We arrive at a nice little bungalow where a family member is waiting outside for us. He is clearly upset but explains that his mother has obviously passed away in the night.

We walk in the house and into the bedroom. It's clear even from the other side of the room that she has passed, but I walk around the bed and touch her anyway. Icy cold skin and signs of rigor mortis when you touch one arm and the whole body sways from side to side like a Weeble it's a fairly safe bet they've gone.

In these situations we have to print off a thirty second ECG trace to give to the police to show there were no signs of life. Anne asked if I was happy doing that bit while she went to talk to the family and explain the ways we would help them and that the police would come along due to it being an 'unexpected death'. Basically give a bit of comfort to them and explain the process in this difficult time.

Meanwhile, in the bedroom, I prepared to put the ECG dots

on the lady and print out a thirty second trace of asystole flatline. I don't know if you know how an ECG machine works and I don't want to teach anyone how to suck eggs. But the short version is, it reads electric signals in the heart. No electric signals equal no wiggly lines on the ECG equals pt has expired! I popped the dots on the very cold and very stiff body of the elderly lady, and nearly shat myself! The line that should have been perfectly flat and smooth was jumping up and down like a toddler after too many Haribos!

From the other room I could hear Anne telling the family that we were very sorry but as they are probably aware she has passed away. Oh fuck! Were there more levels of dead than I knew?

'Errmm Anne, could you pop in here a sec please?'

'I'll be through shortly.'

'Errmm could you come through now just quickly please?'

I heard her excuse herself and walk in. She looked at me with an exasperated expression and said, 'What is it? I'm just trying to console these people, it's not an easy time for them knowing their mum has just passed away.'

'Yeah it's kind of about that actually,' I said as I turned the monitor around to face her. Her eyes went massive and filled the entire lenses of her glasses.

'That's not possible.'

'That's kind of what I thought too! But there it is!'

It was at this point I noticed a small yellow light by the side of the bed. The wire seemed to be going towards the mattress. I reached out and turned off what I now realised was the electric blanket whilst nervously looking at the screen! Flatline! I've since added electric blanket into my checks before confirming anyone is dead!

It's late afternoon on a wintry Saturday and we get a call to the local town centre. I was driving and Colin, my crewmate, was attending. According to the terrafix we were going to a twenty-seven-year-old male with severe abdonomial pains. On arrival he's sitting on a wall and looking very red faced. He's also dribbling a bit!

I pull up along side him.
'You call an ambulance mate?'
He nodded and I gestured towards the back of the vehicle as we pulled over. On getting him in the back we asked him what was going on. He told us that he'd just eaten the country's hottest chilli burger and was now in lots of pain! I know I shouldn't have but this immediately gave me a fit of the giggles and I couldn't look at him without starting again. My crewmate enquired if he was into his spicy food.
'No! I can't stand hot things! My mate dared me and I won a plastic chilli on a key ring!'
This pretty much sent me over the edge and before I knew it someone, who may have been me, was laughing and saying, 'You're such a cock!'
The outburst kind of surprised all three of us as he looked embarrassed and said again. 'My mate dared me.'
This didn't really help and again I repeated, 'You're such a cock.'

We tried our best and took all of his observations, did all of his paperwork and history taking. But I just couldn't keep a

17

straight face as he sat there sweating and burping whilst complaining he didn't like hot food! Eventually he was cleared with the advice that it might be worth him getting some milk or yogurt. And next time don't be such a cock! I like to think he learnt a lesson that day about the correct use for an ambulance. And self-induced eating challenges don't come into that category! I still see Colin now and then and that job always comes up. I'm afraid I still get the giggles every time.

Please don't think that I'm like this with everyone, or that I don't care. Because I really do. But when people are genuinely dying out there and someone has eaten a hot chilli burger for a dare and piece of plastic crap, then I really need to point out that they don't need an ambulance.

I was brought up on a council estate with my parents and older brother. It was known as a bit of a rough estate to others. But we never thought that from the inside. We all knew each other, were all there for each other. But it really was a different time back then with a different ethos to life.

My best mate Gary used to live next door when I was growing up. He was a typical one of those kids who was into everything. 'What do you mean no one can climb up that? Watch this!' 'What do you mean no one can jump down from that far? Hold my 7up!' And nine times out of ten he could do exactly what he said! But on the tenth time there was usually blood! He had a habit of cracking his head open! But it wasn't always his fault, I remember him getting hit on the head with a snowball one year. Which happened to have a massive lump of ice in it! Blood! Played golf with his brother but was standing slightly too close when he swung the club! Blood! Fell off a stool in his kitchen and managed to land on the plate that hit the floor before him! Blood!

But the point I'm making isn't just that I had clumsy friends. It's that we never ever called an ambulance. Because he wasn't dying and we used common sense! His mum didn't drive, but she would put a tea towel over it and come round and ask my dad if he'd mind dropping them to the hospital. Of course, he was more than happy to. It's what you do for friends and neighbours. But even if he wasn't in, I'm pretty sure they would have gotten on a bus with a tea towel over his head rather than call an ambulance!

Saturday night shift and the heavens had opened! The rain was coming down sideways which really wasn't helping with visibility on blue-light drives but we were doing our best. We got a call to a twenty-three-year-old with severe breathing difficulties. It wasn't in our town and was a short drive up the motorway followed by some windy back roads.

This kind of call is categorised as a high importance call meaning, obviously, lights, sirens and a heavy right foot! We pulled up outside the block of flats, grabbed a bag of equipment each as well as our trusty clipboard and in we went. The first thing that hit us was the strong smell of weed! And sure enough laying on the sofa was our 'short of breath' twenty-three-year-old.

'Can we help you mate?' I said whilst hoping we had got the address wrong and I wasn't about to lose my shit with this guy!
'Yeah thanks mate. Can you change my DVD?'

Obviously I'd misheard him; surely no one would be stupid enough to call an emergency ambulance to do something like that. No one is stupid enough to make a crew risk their and others' lives by driving through torrential rain for such a ridiculous reason. Are they?

Apparently they are and that's exactly what he had said as he repeated it again.

'Can you change my DVD?'

My crewmate Percy looked immediately outraged! 'You fuc…'

I put my hand up to silence him. 'Yeah of course we will mate, no trouble at all.'

Percy looked at me like I'd lost my mind. Usually I would be the one to lose it and tell someone exactly what I thought in that situation but here I was agreeing to change the guy's DVD.

I walked over to the tv, crouched down and pushed the eject button on the DVD player. It slid out smoothly and I reached out for the disc. I can only think I must have slipped somehow but the whole DVD tray came off in my hand! 'Oh mate!' I said. 'It's just come off in my hand! There must be a problem with it!'

'You've broken my fucking DVD player!' he shouted at me. As I walked past, dropping it in his lap, I told him he was lucky that's all it was as people were genuinely ill out there! We walked out of the flat back into the dark, wind and rain. We got back in the truck and Percy cracked up laughing.

'That was fucking classic man!'

First day on the road as a qualified paramedic. I was working with a trainee tech and the phone on base went off.

'Hi, we need you to go as paramedic backup on a paediatric

resuscitation, thank you.'

I said OK and hung up. I turned to Nick and said, 'They want paramedic backup for a paediatric resuscitation! Why the hell are they sending? oh fuck!' Realisation suddenly dawned that I was the grown up now and this was all on me.

We got in the truck and, whilst hitting warp factor ten on the way there, found out that it was a four-year-old girl, possible swine flu with a double tech crew on scene.

We soon arrived on scene and got straight to the patient. She was a young Asian girl with a history of asthma. She'd been a bit under the weather anyway. The parents had gone in and found her cold and still, not breathing. They were remarkably calm as we got to work straight away. We already knew what the outcome was going to be but sometimes you just know you're gonna do everything anyway! Even if it's just for the family.

I intubated her and got a cannula in so that we could give potentially life-saving drugs. We told the family we needed to get to the hospital straight away but they decided not to come with us. Extremely strange but people act strangely in these situations. We couldn't stop and debate it and got out to the truck. We called ahead to alert the hospital and continued doing everything we could in the back whilst Nick drove in with a heavy right boot.

Going into resus at A & E can be a surreal experience for a crew. There are a lot of people around and you have to give a full handover to everybody about what's happened and be ready to answer any questions. This is doubled when it's a paediatric. They knew as well as we did that it was futile. But, despite this, did one more round of full CPR with life-saving drug intervention. The doctor in charge looked up, still asystole, is everyone happy to call it, stop working on the patient and declare them dead). He made a point of asking us as the crew who brought her in; I nodded knowing that nothing was going to bring her back.

Due to the possibility of it being swine flu – even though her asthma would have been what made her far more susceptible to it – the hospital wanted to test the rest of the family. Whilst they contacted them, we and the other crew agreed we would go back and get the rest of the family. I ended up travelling in with just the patient's two young brothers in the back of the ambulance with me. For some reason none of the adults chose to come in the truck with the kids. At this point the children didn't know about the outcome of their sister. I was glad it didn't take too long to get to the hospital.

The rest of the family were clear, but there was still one poor little girl who didn't get to see another sunset. Sweet dreams little one.

A midweek day in Brighton and it had been surprisingly quiet. The sun was out, we had been doing a bit of standby at Hove seafront. Standby for those who don't know is when they send us out of base in our ambulances or response cars to stand by at what are considered to be strategic points around the county. This is worked out by the fact that at the exact same time the year before there was an accident near there. Computer says it's right, so I guess it must be right? This, in theory, means that our response times would be quicker and therefore the powers that be would get more tea and medals from the people in the even higher ivory tower than them. So, when you see us at the side of the road, or sitting quietly by the beach in the middle of summer, we really aren't just sitting there checking out the lookers on the sand, we are working! I mean, yes obviously we are looking, but from a purely public safety viewpoint!)

Also, just on the point of standby, this almost never happens now. The ambulance service is absolutely stretched to breaking point, as are all the staff and we just don't get the time to be on standby anywhere. It really can be job to job for the full twelve hours.

The alert goes off and we look at the screen to see where we are going. The job was at a local nursing home so would only take us a few minutes to get there. According to the screen we were attending a male in his eighties who was less responsive than usual today. Within four minutes we were pulling up outside one of the, dare I say, not so great nursing homes in the area. We got our first response bag out along with the heart monitor and obs kit and lugged it all up to the door. We rang the bell and waited. And waited. And then waited a bit more. Eventually someone came to let us in and on the way to the patient's room explained to us that he really wasn't his usual self today. Wasn't interested in his food, hadn't been watching *Bargain Hunt* and hadn't even looked up when his favourite carer went in to say hi.

With our alarm bells going off in our head and spidey senses tingling we arrived at the room and the carer opened the door. Another 'nurse' was sitting on the bed trying to take his blood pressure and said straight away, 'Sorry, I'm having issues with this cuff and can't get a reading.'

I gave her an understanding smile before saying, 'Yes it's

quite often a bit tricky when the patient's dead!'

She looked at me horrified before spinning around and taking a proper look at the patient, who had clearly been dead for a good few hours, before exclaiming, 'He was fine a minute ago!'

As I pointed out, the patient was in fact freezing cold and showing signs of rigor mortis. There were some safeguarding issues to be dealt with and lots of paperwork to be filled out. Funny enough the home was really keen to make us cups of tea with biscuits. But I'm sure they weren't trying to sway our opinion. They wouldn't do that would they?

Be very careful when choosing those nursing homes folks! Not all care homes are created equal.

Growing up I could at times be a right cocky little sod. Was often getting into trouble including lots of things that I'm not gonna write here in case my mum ever reads it; she won't. Like I said, school wasn't really my thing. In fact I hardly ever went for the last two years and preferred instead to go off getting up to all sorts of things. But I also used to go into the greengrocers where I worked at the weekends and do a few hours. My boss figured if I wasn't going to school I was better off there than anywhere else. Somehow, I managed to scrape a few exam passes – thank God for resits – but school just really didn't interest me. But no matter how much of a tearaway I could be, I always had respect for authority figures. I wouldn't dream of gobbing off at an ambulance crew never mind physically trying to assault one. And our local bobby – PC Acton – would definitely not have been given any real reason to remember me by.

New Year's Eve at nearly midnight and it had been a hideously busy night as always. In general New Year's Eve can be an OK night to work. Most people tend to be in fairly good spirits and even the drunk and noisy ones tend to be reasonably good fun and happy to chat rather than aggressive and dangerous. Me and Dan were on our way to a low category job at a pub in town. We were chatting and having a laugh, guessing what this would turn out to be. Suddenly over the radio we heard a 'code ' twenty activation. A code twenty was an activation when someone hit their crew down button. It indicates that they are in potential danger and are requesting immediate back up. This used to be put out over the radio as an 'all call' so that any crew in the area could call up and respond to it. It would then also be put through to the police who would attend if able. But sometimes we were closer. They have done away with this all call activation now which I guess is down to health and safety. The call still gets put through to the police but local crews aren't made aware in order to be able to go and assist. Although a good dispatcher who knows certain crews may ask if you are willing to 'drive by' if you happen to be close by.

The call went out stating, 'Crew in trouble in Southwick – a nearby town – with a group of youths attacking them and the ambulance. Any nearby responders available?' I was driving but immediately hit my call button. 'Crew calling go ahead.'

'We can be at the code twenty in under ten minutes.'

'But aren't you in Lancing?' Lancing is two towns away but I was feeling confident and we will always put our foot down to help someone else in our 'green family'; the name we in the ambulance service give to our fellow colleagues.

'Yes, yes. On our way.' The dispatcher knew my colleague

and I and I'm guessing this is why they didn't argue and let us continue on our way at speed.

I should probably mention that neither myself nor my colleague are small lads and both know how to look after ourselves. A fact that was well known amongst certain members of control who would be happy to send us to certain things that they may not choose to send to everyone.

We hammered over the dual carriageway as quick as we could – obviously obeying all road laws and restrictions given to us, your honour! – and we were soon just round the corner from the incident. We made sure our sirens were wailing away to let the crew know help was on the way as well as letting the assailants know that another emergency service was close by. I think we were still sideways when we flew round the corner into the road seeing the ambulance ahead of us and I think we were both halfway out of the doors before the vehicle had come to a stop. The large group of teenagers looked up and instantly started running away as the pair of us flew towards them.

Our colleague from the other crew – an older gent who had been there and seen it all – and his female crew mate both got out of the truck laughing.

'Evening boys,' he said. 'Don't take this personally but I've never been this pleased to see you two.'

It turned out that they had originally been called out to one of the lads who was not really responding to his friends and may or may not have taken something other than drink. On arriving the lad had just been a bit drunk and told them to fuck off. Not an unusual occurrence in our line of work. When they pointed out there was no need for that and they had only attended because they had been called the lads all decided to join in and get a bit shouty and aggressive. Turns out they weren't so brave when reinforcements turned up.

This used to be a pretty rare thing for crews to be attacked but unfortunately the years have seen this happen more and more. In 2020 alone there were two hundred and forty-five cases of physical harm against members of South East Coast Ambulance Service alone. As well as two hundred and nineteen reported instances of verbal abuse towards staff. I can guarantee you that there would have been a hell of a lot more cases of both that were never reported. And this is what I don't understand. Violence or aggression against anyone trying to help you just seems like madness to me. Don't get me wrong, I know that when people are scared, hurting or worried for family members they can act very out of character but I would say it's likely that these aren't the ones reported. Some people just want to fight and have no care about who it's with.

Brighton Pride!

Have you ever been? You really should! The city is descended on by thousands of extra people all coming down to join in the festivities. Brighton is always a very cosmopolitan place that welcomes everyone of every shape, size, colour, gender or anything else you can imagine.

But during pride that goes into overdrive! The whole place is a sea of colour and the most extravagant and sometimes minimalist outfits that you can imagine.

Want a dwarf in full dominatrix outfit? Seen one. A six feet nun with muscles, tattoos and a beard? Seen one. A six feet five black transvestite on twelve-inch platform heels and a neon minidress covered in fairy lights? Not even a rarity! And man they can walk on those heels like they are gliding! Great legs too!

Anyway, it was a sunny pride Saturday and me and Pauline were cruising through Brighton in a bright yellow ambulance. We'd been having a good laugh as we always did. She was good fun to work with and it had been a good day so far with pretty chilled, nice patients.

It was a lovely warm day and the windows were down, shades on, arm resting on the open window ledge. We were watching all the fantastic outfits as the people walked along the street. We stopped at traffic lights and chatted when I felt someone next to me. The view that met me when I turned round was a young good-looking guy with a six-pack wearing red sequinned hot pants, red sequinned cowboy boots and devil's horns. He gave me a big smile before lovingly saying, 'Fancy a fuck?' I honestly thought Pauline was gonna choke from the mad laughter that suddenly came from the driver's side! She was crying!

I looked at him and smiled while saying, 'Oh, ermm, thanks very much. But, I just had one!' Which started her off even more!

He gave me a big smile before joining his friends before carrying on.

I don't know if you are familiar with the centre of Brighton, but the lights are about every fifty metres apart. And sure enough we stopped again before they had even reached them on foot. Despite my protests of 'Put the fucking lights on and just drive through!' Pauline, who was still killing herself laughing by the way, refused. Red pants saw and instantly came beaming over to the side of the truck.

'How about now?'

I'm surprised we didn't need an inco pad for Pauline's seat!

Starting out on emergency ambulances as a trainee technician can be really hard. For a while there is that feeling of being completely unprepared. No amount of training can prepare you for the things you are going to see. Or even more difficult, the things you're going to feel. If you are lucky enough you get a good regular paramedic crewmate who you can learn from and allows you to expand your skills and knowledge, pushes you to do things you aren't entirely comfortable doing. Because that's how you learn and become what you need to be.

Then you get relief week! This is where you fill in other gaps in the rota for sickness and holidays and means you work with a variety of people. This can be really good as you get to see how other people work and teaches you to adapt your approach to things. There's often more than one way to crack an egg!

However, it can also lead to knocks in your confidence and self-doubts if you happen to end up with someone who doesn't want to teach or help. Or maybe just expects you to know and do everything right from the start. Or maybe they make decisions that you aren't entirely happy with. And even the most confident of us can find it difficult to override the decision of a very experienced medic.

Three months in as a trainee technician and I'm working with Simon. He's a big, gruff guy with twenty-eight years in the service where he's also a union rep. He's not a very friendly guy

29

towards me and I was desperately trying to find some common ground. Something to talk about to make this twelve-hour shift feel less like a twenty-four-hour shift. It was a cold and wet Friday night. Two jobs done so far and I'm already feeling pretty miserable. He's not someone who was known for his work ethic and would do his best to avoid what he could.

We get a call to a lady in her late seventies with chest pain in a block of flats in Brighton. It was my turn to attend. We park up outside and walk along the long pavement up to the block before climbing one flight of stairs to the patient's door. I knocked the door and waited as we heard the pt shuffling towards it. Eventually an elderly lady opened it. She looked very pale and I introduced ourselves and said, 'Let's sit you down and do some observations while you tell us what's been happening.' I held out the bag of equipment that we had brought with us as if to emphasise the point.

'Tell you what,' said Simon, 'let's get you down in the ambulance and we will do it all there.'

I gave him a bit of a concerned look as I felt the best option would be to get an ECG on her before we went anywhere. Not only would this show us if there were any serious cardiac issues going on but also let us know if we needed to pre alert the hospital or even take her somewhere different.

'Excuse my colleague,' he said, 'he's new!'

I managed to choke back my anger and the response I would have given if a patient hadn't been there. 'I'll go and get the chair.' It was best practice that a cardiac patient was not made to walk anywhere putting extra strain on a possibly already injured heart. And especially not down a flight of stairs and across a large frontage before even reaching the ambulance on a cold wet winter's evening.

'It's OK, we don't need the chair. We'll just have a little slow stroll down there. No rush.' I looked at him like he had two heads and again indicated our clearly poorly lady. 'It's fine!' he said again, a bit more forcefully. 'We will just take it slowly.'

'Simon I really think we should get the chair, I'm more than happy to get it myself.' Protocol states that the attendant, in this case me, stays with the patient while the driver goes for the chair. But I knew that wasn't happening!

'I said it's fine, we don't need it!' he snapped. 'You are going to worry this lady. She can lean on us and will be fine!'

I felt so angry, but also so completely out of my depth. How could I, the brand new trainee tech, go against this very experienced paramedic union rep? Who was going to listen to me over him?

I absolutely knew I was right. I also knew that I was against an immovable object and further arguments would only lead to further delay for the patient. And I guess if I'm completely honest, I knew it would make my long night even worse.

We slowly walked her down the stairs with me asking every other step if she was OK and sure she could manage it. My crewmate continuously answering that she was fine and doing great. After what seemed like forever we got to the ambulan ce and got her up the two steps into the back. I got her straight onto the trolley and as I looked at my colleague, who I expected to be passing me the leads to assess her heart rhythm or preparing to take her blood pressure or maybe even getting a cannula into her arm in case we needed to give drugs on the way, but no, he looked at me before walking down the steps and saying 'I'll be in the front, shout when you're ready to go,' and slamming the door.

I was gobsmacked. I wanted to drag him back in by his neck and tell him to do his bloody job! But instead I turned my attention to my patient who was looking decidedly unwell. I explained what I was doing as I put a probe on her finger to measure her oxygen levels and heart rate, attached a blood pressure cuff to her arm and then started putting the ECG dots onto her chest.

I looked at the very rapid lines on the monitor for about thirty seconds before she arrested. I banged hard on the window separating the cab from the rear saloon. 'Simon, get your arse back here!' I instantly hit the lever that dropped the back of the stretcher flat. The bump as it landed flat acted as a precordial thump and her heart started again.

Finally the back door opened. 'What?'

'She arrested you twat!' I said which was a lot calmer and more polite than I was feeling.

He looked at the clearly unwell patient and then the heart monitor which was now beating fairly steadily, although not as much as I would have liked. 'You sure? Looks OK.' I can only assume it was the expression on my face and the clenching of my fists that made him say that OK maybe he needed to go in the back and I could put my foot down in the front.

Well, put my foot down I did. It's always a fine line in an ambulance as we need to get to hospital quickly whilst remembering someone is working in the back. But before long we arrived at the hospital. I jumped out and ran round the back, opened the door to find nothing happening. No sense of urgency, no new observations done en route, he hadn't even cannulated the patient.

Now I don't know if he genuinely didn't believe that the patient had arrested and as such didn't feel he needed to do more regardless I would have done another set of observations and cannulated the patient or as I suspect he's just a lazy work-shy waste of space who should have stopped pulling the uniform on many years ago.

After we had checked the patient in I went to the loo to calm down. Finally I walked back out to find him standing with another older ambulance colleague with a cuppa in his hand.

'Did you get me one?'

'Oh, I didn't know you wanted one,' he said.

It's fair to say that the rest of the night was a quiet one. And I was lucky enough not to have to work with him again.

I know I should have reported him that night. I know that if it had been even a year later I would have torn into him for his behaviour and reported him straight away. But this is what I mean about it being tough starting out. I was convinced that nobody would listen to a brand new out of the pack trainee tech against him. The ambulance service has, over the years, had a bit of a bullying history and looked out for the 'old boys club'. It still happens now but possibly not as obviously as it used to.

I often still think about that lady even now twenty years later. I wonder if she ever got to leave hospital. And how many other patients had he treated in that same way. I wish I had been stronger at the time or just called control and said I needed another crew as my crewmate was refusing to help. But it probably would have finished my time at that station before it even got started.

I may have mentioned but I'm not a small bloke. I'm quite a big solid guy with two sleeve tattoos. In a bad mood I know that I can look quite scary. Which is probably why people find the fact that I'm terrified of spiders so funny! Seriously, run at me with a knife and I'd probably deal with it fairly calmly. Run at me with a spider and I'm gonna scream like a girl before legging it in the other direction.

Another nightshift, me and Percy find ourselves getting sent to a nursing home. Not an unusual occurrence by any stretch of the imagination. If I'm completely honest I can't even remember what the job was, but the patient needed to be taken into hospital. Percy was attending so I headed down and got the carry chair – our small foldable chair that we use to extricate non-walking patients from their houses and often up and down stairs. The amount of stairs is usually directly proportionate to how heavy the patient is! The heavier the patient, the more stairs they will be up.) from the ambulance. I brought it back up and we lifted the patient across onto the chair. As always we wrapped her up warmly in blankets as it was a cold night outside and I explained that I was going to tilt the chair back onto its two rear wheels in order to get her out of the home. The door was partly open and I headed towards it, which was when a spider the size of a ford escort ran across the floor in front of me blocking my path out of the room. This may sound dramatic but trust me I wasn't walking past while it was just sitting there staring at me!
Percy looked at me and a big grin appeared across his face.

'Move that bloody thing out of the way,' I said.

'Oh come on, it's only a little spider,' he replied. It wasn't little! I could see the tattoos up all of its arms and its teeth as it grinned at me.)

'Get it out of the bloody way now or I'm not going anywhere!' I said in a slightly stronger tone that indicated my big swear words were not gonna be far behind.

Laughing to himself and at me Percy swung the door further open and the brush along the bottom of it pushed the spider away and left the route clear for me. I grabbed the back of the chair and almost ran with my patient through it, Percy still laughing behind me as the spider pushed the door shut whilst probably telling us to 'come and have a go if you think you're hard enough!'

Later that same night and after much joyful piss-taking from my crewmate and every other crew we bumped into who were quickly told by my crewmate, we were given a transfer to London. We used to get quite a few of these for various reasons. Quite often it would be to various special care baby units due to lack of space. A lot of crews didn't like getting them but we loved them. It would take you out of area for a change of scenery and could take up a lot of your shift. But that was always good getting out and about for a change.

We were on our way back after dropping the patient at hospital and doing a bit of sightseeing around London, having a bit of a laugh whilst heading back to hopefully get a late break and a bit of guaranteed down time. Percy was driving at the time and suddenly had a very panicked expression on his face.

'Get it out, fucking get that thing out of the way, it flew at me.'

This was when I noticed for the first time a moth that had obviously come into the cab somewhere along the way and was now flapping itself against his head repeatedly.

'That spider's not fucking funny now, is it sunshine?' I said chuckling away to myself as I leant over, caught the moth in my hands, and let it free out of the window.

He didn't seem to take the piss as much after that bit of the journey, funny enough.

I would love to tell you confidently that this was the only time that a spider has ever caused me problems in the line of duty. However this would be a complete and utter bare-faced lie. So here goes.

We were at a resus and I have to be honest and say I can't even remember who my crewmate was at the time. I think the traumatic events of the day have made me erase it from my mind. No not the resus, the spider! I remember it was mid-afternoon in a beautiful big house. An elderly male had collapsed on the upstairs landing and was no longer breathing. I was running – leading – the resus and had taken care of the airway and cannulated the patient whilst my crewmate was doing compressions. Another crew had joined us as is ideal on a resus due to the strenuous nature of the job as well as the need to be doing many things at once sometimes. More hands as well as more mental input is always a good thing in this case.

In order to keep chest compressions effective it is best practice to keep swapping positions so that you don't depend on one person who will tire very quickly. Even when you think you are still OK it's amazing how quick the efficacy of compressions can drop off.

Anyway, it was my turn to do compressions and with the sun blazing through the windows it wasn't taking long to get a bit of a sweat on. As the sweat dripped into my eyes I thought I saw something moving across the floor out the corner of my eye. I rubbed my face on the sleeve of my shirt as I continued and looked up again. Just as the big spider crawled under my patient. Oh my god! There was nearly two of us on the floor. Suddenly I was hit with a horrible dilemma. If this resus was successful, as of course we always want them to be, then we would be needing to pick this man up and put him on our ambulance. That meant I was going to be in very close contact with the eight legged monster very soon. Unless...

'Rich, do you want me to take over on those compressions for a bit?'

'Oh, it's OK mate, I'll just do one more round then we'll change over.'

They were probably the best compressions I'd ever done and anything under that poor gentleman was getting squashed!

Unfortunately, despite our best efforts, and even with the monster underneath him we really did do our best; we were on this occasion unsuccessful and due to the death being unexpected we were asked by the police to leave the gentleman in place for the coroner to view. So no running and screaming from me!

A cold and rainy night and it had already felt like quite a long one. I was working alone on the car and I'd been from job to job. Sometimes as a first responder and other times to back up crews in order to give further drugs or pain relief. I got a 'cause for concern' job. This is when a family member may have not heard from a relative for quite some time and they can't get any answer either from the house or from a phone call. I'm not sure why but these always seem to happen in the middle of the night. I mean, who is calling their elderly relatives at one in the morning and then being worried that they didn't answer the phone?

Anyway, the house was in the middle of nowhere and it had been a reasonable drive to it. A couple of minutes before arriving control updated me with a keysafe code on my on-board computer. This meant that if there was still no answer I could at least let myself in where I would walk round the house shouting 'hello, ambulance, is anyone here?' at the top of my voice while pretending to be brave and hoping no mad murderer ran at me in the dark.

Eventually, I found the isolated house in the middle of the woods and parked up. I got out of the car, grabbed my first response bag and obs kit and walked up to the door. I rang the doorbell and knocked the door loudly like one of those delivery men that wake you up and then leg it with your parcel before you get to the door three seconds later. I tried this a few times and waited for some kind of response. The one I wanted was someone turning lights on to prewarn me before coming to the door saying 'It's the middle of the bloody night what are you doing?' However, as I expected I was met with darkness and silence. It's OK, I thought, I have the keysafe code. So I walked to the side of the entrance porch where I found the keysafe. With a fucking great tarantula on it! I mean literally, right on the buttons that I needed to push to open it.

OK, so obviously it wasn't a real tarantula, but my god it

was huge! It had boots on all of its feet and was smoking a pipe while holding a can of Tennant's Special Brew. And I was on my own! I can't emphasise enough how much I don't like spiders. But I had a moment of panic. How the hell am I supposed to get in the house now? I had a bit of an internal battle going on in my head. What if the patient was stuck on the floor with a broken hip?

Yeah but the big spider is stopping me getting in!

What if the patient is lying on the floor breathing their last breath?

Yeah but the big spider is stopping me getting in!

What if you're just acting like a big girl and you need to just do this?

Yeah but the spider!

I looked at this thing again, standing on the keypad, daring me to try and use it with its red fangs gleaming at me. I wonder if I can call for back up? Hmm, could be a tricky conversation with control. As I stood there pondering these terrifying dilemmas the mammoth spider moved. I didn't scream, but I definitely made a high pitched noise and jumped four feet backwards. It was almost like it had decided to stop playing with me and moved up to the top of the keysafe off of the numbers. I still definitely wasn't brave enough to just push them in case it suddenly ran back down and bit me. So I got my small pen torch out and using the extra length of that pushed the code quicker than anyone ever had done in their life. The front sprang forward like I'd finished a challenge on *The Crystal Maze,* and I quickly grabbed the key before running back to the front door.

I stopped by the front door, key in hand and panting like I'd just run a marathon. I opened the door and walked slowly into the house hitting the light switch as I went. 'Hello, ambulance,' I shouted at the top of my voice. 'Is anyone here?' Silence. I walked around the downstairs opening every door and shouting the same thing, before starting to climb the stairs with my heart in my mouth.

It doesn't matter how many times you've done this before it always gets the adrenaline going. What are you going to find? Is the patient going to be OK? Is the patient going to have quietly passed in the night? What if the patient isn't there at all and it is a crazed killer who has escaped from a nearby asylum under a dastardly pseudonym and is now waiting for our hapless hero to arrive? Yes, OK, I know it's unlikely but your mind really does get carried away at times!

Eventually, I got to the top and started the whole thing again of opening every door, shouting out the whole time. Checking behind the doors, down the sides of the bed, in the wardrobes – it has been known I promise – and everywhere else just to check you haven't missed anything. The crescendo of your heart rate getting higher with every door you open, knowing that the odds of the patient or axe murderer being in the next room are very high. Until eventually you open the last door! And there's no one there! The whole house is empty. Being thorough you have a quick check in the back garden before eventually locking the house up, facing a spider the size of a Ford Fiesta to put the key back in the safe and messaging control. Nothing found!

I don't know if they have any idea of quite how much your heart is in your mouth as they reply with 'OK, stand down,' before instantly sending another job straight through to your terrafix.

OK, I promise that's the last spider related story!

Another nightshift and I was on ambulance with Jolene. Another crewmate that I only worked with occasionally but always got on well with and you could guarantee having a laugh. Apart from the fact she was a bit scared of the dark. And loud noises. And being on her own in the dark.

It had been a good shift so far, reasonably busy but all pretty good natured patients and nothing we couldn't handle. We'd been having a good laugh when the dreaded 'cause for concern' came through. We drove to a nice road in Hove actually and pulled up outside a large house. It was, as always, the early hours of the morning as we got out of the ambulance and walked up the drive with Jolene telling me not to leave her alone. We rang the doorbell and knocked loudly at the door then waited a few minutes before doing it again, listening hard for any movement inside or signs of the curtains moving before agreeing that there was definitely no response.

We had no keysafe for this address so I told Jolene to stay where she was out the front which was a bit better lit up with street lights and said I would walk round the back of the house to see if anything was unlocked. She wasn't too keen on the idea of staying out front alone. But then she wasn't particularly any keener on walking around the back of the house where it was darker and we had no idea what we were likely to find. She decided to wait where she was.

I walked down the dark side passage round to the back of the house. There was a large well-manicured garden but no signs of anyone lying on the floor out there so I walked over to the back of the house and a pair of large patio doors. I tried looking through the nets but it was just too dark and purely on a whim thought I'd try the patio door. Which slid open soundlessly in my hand. I thought about going back round the front to get Jolene before going in but then remembered that the last time I'd walked through an empty house with her I ended up with nail marks in my arm. So, I decided I would go through the house, turning the lights on and shouting out until I got to the front door. I put my hand inside the doors and felt for a light switch, before realising that it would be through this room and by the door rather than at the back door. Really wishing I'd taken a proper torch with me I reached for my trusty penlight. This probably gave me about three inches of semi-usable light. Not ideal.

I called out loudly 'Ambulance service! Is anyone here?' before slowly stepping into the room, looking like Mr Magoo squinting to see further than a couple of inches ahead. I was leaning forwards and sweeping the tiny beam of light from left to right just in case I saw anything. I clattered into an upright piano due to not being able to see it until the very last minute and let out a couple of quiet swear words under my breath. I moved round it and carried on before exclaiming, not quietly, 'FUCK!' as literally three inches in front of my face appeared a pair of eyes. I very nearly dropped the pen torch as well as very nearly dropping my lunch from earlier. In an upright chair sat the patient. Clearly very dead. I'm not quite sure why but to double check I poked him in the forehead whilst saying 'hello?' I'm not quite sure what response I would have expected from this if he had been alive but it just seemed the right thing to do at the time.

I moved past him to the doorway where I turned on the light before going back to him. Poor old man had obviously died some time earlier in the day. He was still sitting upright in his chair. Very rigored and very cold. I made my way to the front door and opened it, which made Jolene jump.

'Have you found him?' she said.

'Yep,' I answered before leading her into the house so that we could officially confirm death and fill in the required paperwork.

Brighton could be a great place to work. It's just the most cosmopolitan of places where absolutely anything goes. You see every type of person and in the summer it's just rammed. Thousands of people descend on the city from family holiday makers, stag or hen dos – Seen some sights on these believe me! I'm fairly sure I'll tell you one or two of them at some point – as well as the day trippers who fancy a day at the seaside or the local bars at the last minute.

It's also like a beacon to many, many homeless people who seem to make their way to the streets of the seaside city. As of December 2021 there were estimated to be at least three thousand, seven hundred homeless people on the streets of Brighton. Unfortunately for many different reasons there isn't always a happy ending for these people with many falling to drugs, drink or just poor health due to their living conditions.

Due to the sheer amount of people and lifestyles it can also, at times, be a lonely place. And I'm sure many people go unnoticed for a long time before people realise they aren't going to be seen again.

Another sunny day in Brighton and I was in a response car. It had been fairly steady so far with a few minutes to chill between jobs and the odd bit of standby down at Hove seafront watching the world go by. A job came through for a 'cause for concern' at a flat along Hove seafront. A lot of the properties in Brighton and Hove consist of what were once quite grand houses that have over the years been broken down into flats and in some cases bedsits to fit even more in. I turned up outside one such place and rang on the doorbell where the young man from the downstairs flat led me into his living room whilst telling me hadn't seen the elderly lady from upstairs for quite some time. However he was concerned that she had left something on in her flat as the dark patch on his ceiling had been growing and this morning started to drip slightly through onto his floor. He wasn't very happy and had tried getting hold of her but had no luck. She was definitely going to get a piece of his mind when he saw her about the mess on the ceiling and also the stench from her flat.

As I looked up I was just thinking to myself that he probably didn't have enough spare to give anyone a piece of his mind.

I advised him to stay in his flat and that I would go and have a look to find out what was going on. On my way up I called control and advised them that I would need to gain entry into the flat and my reasons for doing so. With every step upwards the stench got worse and as I stood outside the front door of the flat it was pretty awful. I knocked a few times and called out although

I already knew that nobody was going to answer and then I forced the front door.

I'm lucky enough to be blessed with a pretty poor sense of smell. But even so it hit me like a bag of skunks! I could see straight into the living room which had the sun blazing through the big windows on this beautiful summer's day and straight onto the now decomposing and melting body of the poor elderly lady. I couldn't even give you an idea as to how long she had been there unnoticed and alone, but she was now stuck to the carpet, the breakdown of her body as fats melted into fluids and then slowly causing a stain on the ceiling of the flat downstairs before eventually dripping onto the angry young man below.

I've always had a fairly strong stomach but I have to say that job tested it to its max! However, no lunch was spilt on the carpet. Well, not mine anyway!

I spent a lot of time thinking about that poor old lady afterwards. How long had she been there? Why hadn't she been missed? Did she have no family, or just none that cared about her? Like I say, Brighton can be a lonely place at times and it is easy, as I guess it is anywhere, to be forgotten about.

If you don't take anything else from this book then please just take this, check on each other. Check on your elderly neighbours or the quiet ones who don't know how to meet your eye when you pass in the hallway or your paths. If you haven't seen your little old neighbours for a while, just give 'em a knock and check they are OK. I know it's an inconvenience for you. But even if it's not life and death for them, you could really make someone's week by showing you care enough to ask.

Anyway, I got a little bit sentimental and serious there! I wouldn't want you to think I was starting to care too much!

Back in the 'old days' before the morale police joined the ambulance service we used to be able to have a bit of fun. There were lots of pranks played between crews to helps us through what could at times be a tough day. It started with the crew room banter we used to have and carried on to pranks out on the road. As a young technician I was working with a much older experienced paramedic who was known for being a bit straight faced. We were at a patient who had a problem with her hip and would need to go to hospital. But before we moved her anywhere she needed some pain relief. He barked at me that he would need the drugs bag and cannulation kit which I was already on my way out to get. He knew that was what I was doing but was one of those people who had to show everyone that he was in charge by barking orders out. I walked out to the truck, enjoying a couple of minutes of sunshine, got the kit we needed and walked back in. Obviously, he moaned that I had taken too long – I hadn't – and that I was slowing things up for this poor lady; I wasn't.

I put the bag down next to him and moved back slightly. Most people you work with see things as a team effort and are happy for whoever is with them to start getting things set up for them, personally I think it's a big help and confidence boost if you let the newer members of staff get things ready as they feel much more comfortable doing things when you need them quickly then. However some people insist that they are attending and therefore should be doing everything and it is not your job to touch the patient. Back in the day as a youngster it was a bit upsetting. These days it's fun to watch them flapping like mad when you could quite easily help them out.

Anyway, he scowled at me and grabbed the bag whilst apologising to the patient that she had needed to wait so long, I literally went to the end of the path and back, I didn't leave the country whilst the lovely lady repeated that she thought I'd been very quick and thanked me again. He looked even more unhappy at this as he scowled first at her and then me before ripping the zip open on the drugs bag. The look on his face as four porno mags fell out of it and onto the floor was something I will never forget for as long as I live.

The patient immediately saw they almost landed on her, so unavoidable really and started laughing whilst her husband made noises similar to Sid James in a *Carry On* film, over in the corner of the room. When a situation requires someone not to laugh then I promise you, I am not the person you want standing there. I think my attempt to stifle it for a minute before it came out ended up in a loud raspberry noise before I broke into a proper fit of giggles. To his credit he actually cracked a smile and said the guys on station had stitched him up and they honestly weren't his. It broke the tension and relaxed the patient whilst she was then cannulated and given pain relief for her trip to hospital. She then proceeded to tell every single person we saw in the hospital all about it while my crewmate looked more and more angry.

When we left the hospital I thought his head was going to explode. I never did find out who put them there but I promise it wasn't me. I wish it had been though as they missed a treat not being there to see his face.

Some other classics were hypoGel on the door handle, man that stuff stuck like the proverbial shit to a blanket! Once it was on your hands then pretty much everything was gonna be sticky that day, no matter how many times you washed them. Another favourite was squirting a large syringe full of water into your crewmate's lap just as you arrived at a job. The moment of clarity as they felt the liquid soaking through and realised they still had to get out and deal with the patient despite the fact they looked like a toddler who'd had too much juice.

One of the guys came into the station one day with a large jade green clock shaped like a mosque. His brother had been to Morocco and decided that it would be a great gift for him. He took one listen to the alarm and knew it had to go straight to the ambulance station. When the alarm went off on this clock it was the traditional call to prayer – I actually really like that sound – but my word it was loud. We were based opposite a fire station and if it went off they would be able to hear it if the windows were open. We had months of fun with that clock, hiding it everywhere we could think of so the alarm would go off at random times of the day or night meaning whoever was on station had to find it and turn it off if they wanted any peace. Believe me, it wasn't a thirty second alarm, it went on for ages. We hid it in cupboards, under the reclining seats, in the space above the ceiling tiles and just waited for it to go off and be found. You wouldn't think we could have such fun with a cheap jade green clock!

A summer's day and I was working with Claude. It was a proper windows down type of day and we were working on our arms out of the window tan. We'd been back on station for a short while and got a call to a resus in a doorway of a block of flats in the next town. The town in particular, like many towns, had a slightly dodgy area to it. That's exactly where we were headed. Lots of high-rise flats in close proximity to each other and not the most pleasant of occupants.

We cut our way through the traffic in the bright sunshine whilst discussing what we were going to and if anyone else had been sent to assist. With a resuscitation more hands make for an easier job as there are more people to assist with chest compressions, drug administration and dealing with the airway, not to mention getting more kit from the truck and getting things ready for when we need to move the patient. We were told by control that we were going to be the first vehicle there and to call them with an early update of the situation and what other help we needed.

As we pulled round the corner into the close, windows still open, we saw a crowd of people outside the doorway of one of the blocks of flats. We turned off our sirens and stopped about twenty feet away. They all turned and looked at us, waving like mad to show us the patient just for information, we would have found them anyway, he was in the middle of all the people on the floor, there really was no need to keep waving, and we opened the doors to jump round and get the kit out of the back. And that's when it started! The prayer clock! It seemed even louder in the afternoon sun with all those people watching as the call shouted out from our ambulance. Those not already staring at us certainly did now. Claude and I looked at each other absolutely mortified yet at the same time trying not to laugh as we opened the back of the truck. I know we both had a quick scan for the clock as we grabbed our kit out before going over to the patient. But as I already knew would be the case, neither of us could see it within arm's reach. So this is how we ended up doing a full resus in the doorway of a block of flats whilst the call to prayer continued at top volume behind us!

It didn't help unfortunately!

A big part of being in the ambulance service is all about spatial awareness. We go to a lot of houses that haven't seen a Hoover in a while. A long while. And that's not even including the houses we go to belonging to the known drug dealers or users. The last thing you want to do is kneel on something that could cause you significant injury and even long term future issues. As well as this a lot of our work is outside. It's not always easy to see everything around you at two a.m. in a dark alleyway while it's absolutely pissing it down and everyone is shouting at you to do something. But that just makes it all the more important to remain calm, look around you and have a systematic approach. Rather than rushing in all excitable and potentially kneeling on a needle or some other nasty.

A cold windy evening and I was working with a new trainee tech. If you happen to be reading this then I can only apologise for the fact I don't remember who it was. That's not anything against you. Just an indication of my brain being addled after twenty-five years on ambulances.

We got called to an old gentleman who was basically feeling a bit unwell. Non-specific illness. Not unusual as often people can't be specific about what's going on or how they are feeling.

Unless you have bits hanging off that shouldn't be or stuff on the outside that should be on the inside it can be difficult to pinpoint things at times.

On the way to the job my crewmate, whose turn it was to attend, was excitedly guessing what it could be. I explained that we would soon find out if we took a stepwise approach to his condition. Count out the bad things and work our way down. But just to be calm and not rush. As soon as we arrived he was off like a whippet. Almost running up the path and into the living room. I stood back taking a good overall look at the scene as he knelt on the floor by the patient who was sitting upright on the sofa. He started asking the patient what was wrong and the patient explained he just didn't feel right. The patient told him that he was usually very well and had no medical conditions. Whilst my crewmate was telling him how amazing it was that he was normally so well I pointed out the almost pharmacy measures of medication on the side and proceeded to read them out and explain what they were for.

To cut a long story short – because I can't think of anything else funny that happened at that job – he basically was on old man on his own who just wanted a bit of company for a while. This really isn't that unusual and I've got all the time in the world for these people who are just genuinely low and lonely. He didn't want to waste our time or be a nuisance. He just wanted someone to care for a little while.

We chatted with him for a while, my crewmate sitting at his feet like a doting puppy and I made him a cup of tea. Then eventually it was time to go. We wished him well, messaged his

GP about a few little issues he had and to try to arrange some kind of care package for him and then left. I watched my crewmate get up carefully from the floor and almost limp outside. I turned to him as we shut the door and looked at his legs.

'You OK?'

'Sort of,' he said. 'When I knelt down I knelt in piss! I was too embarrassed to move or make a fuss so I sat in it for the rest of the time we were there.'

'Oh!' I said. 'Yeah I saw that before you knelt down,' as I erupted into fits of laughter.

'You bastard!' he said. 'I can't believe you didn't tell me before I knelt in it.'

'We've all done it,' I said. 'But usually only once! I reckon you'll look before you kneel down for the rest of your career now!'

See! Spatial awareness! It's not just there for the pointy things in life!

Radio advert comes on in the kitchen: 'You'll feel so much better when you stop smoking!'

Me: 'Especially if you've been on fire for a while!'

Wife: Disapproving look.

Reminder to self: Inside voice!

You see, this is what the job does to us. We don't see things the way 'normal' non-job people do. We develop a very dark sense of humour, things that most people wouldn't even think of, never mind actually say. We don't say any of it with malice, although I'm sure to some people it could seem that way. It's a coping mechanism. A way of making sure we can get up tomorrow and deal with the same horrific things that we've managed to get through today.

Ambulance staff humour is definitely not for the dinner table! Unless the other guests were also ambulance staff, or police. I was going to add fire service to this but they would probably be sleeping or working their second jobs. Only joking water fairies, we love you really. I've lost count of the amount of times I've gone to give a quick answer to something and remembered just in time that I'm not around work colleagues but actually with normal people. Or worse still, the times I've said it before I've realised and it's only been the appalled shocked faces that made me realise I'd forgotten my surroundings.

There are lots of these fly on the wall programmes nowadays on the ambulances or with the police. There is no way in the world I'd be happy having one of those cameras in the cab with me. Some of the subjects we discuss in a shift are really not for the faint-hearted and I would never want them to be shared with or released upon the poor unsuspecting general public. But again, please remember, it's just how we get through the day. We can go to the most horrific of incidents and be making jokes about similar subjects within minutes. We genuinely don't find these things funny. But we have to find a way to normalise it in order to be able to live this career out. Because the last thing you want is us freezing if we ever see anything like it again because we never managed to get past the previous incident.

This is another time where a good crewmate is worth their weight in gold. For twelve hours you are trapped in a metal box with someone. And twelve hours can either go quickly, or very,

very, VERY slowly. I'm lucky enough to have been blessed over the years with some great crewmates who became very good mates. I had complete trust in them and knew that it would be an enjoyable shift. You know what a great crewmate you have when everything just appears as you need it. They pre-empt everything you need and know what you are about to do next. Nothing makes the day more manageable than working with someone you consider a good mate.

Going out to a shout on an ambulance isn't always about treating the patient as such. Sometimes there are times that this is no longer possible. But the people on scene need you to be there for them. And even just go through the motions of doing everything despite knowing that it isn't going to work.

A cold rainy evening and Colin and I were working together. We got on well but I think the weather had just taken the energy out of the pair of us. It was a properly grim night and we just wanted to be in our homes with our families. The terrafix buzzed into life and we both saw a job that made the night instantly worse. One-year-old baby, not breathing. I was driving and went straight into full on race-driver mode. Hammering it through the streets, cutting through traffic and doing anything I could to make up any extra seconds that I could to get us there and hopefully save a life.

At the back of our minds was the hope that we would arrive to hear the little one crying and know that it wasn't as it initially sounded. We turned up at the house and could hear the distraught crying of mum straight away. We ran in and mum had her baby boy in her arms, we could see straight away that he had gone. But there is no way we would ever say that or even think it. We instantly let training over and started doing our best to resuscitate him whilst the parents cried behind us. We talked to them as much as we could at the same time, trying to get a history of what had happened. Mum had gone in to check on him as he had been unwell during the day to find him very cold and blue in his cot. A second crew turned up and helped the parents get everything together that we could take to the hospital, all the baby's information, and started giving them things to do in order to help give them purpose and distraction at such a hideously tragic time. We pre alerted the hospital about what we were coming in with and my crewmate drove us to hospital as quickly as he could whilst I continued doing my best for the patient. We both knew it wasn't going to happen. But that didn't mean we tried any less or felt any less heartbroken for it. We arrived at hospital and as expected it was called quite quickly and death announced.

It's at times like this that we feel more helpless than any other. At the time my son was around the same age. As much as we try to disassociate from the patient and to keep our own lives separate, sometimes it's inevitable. We are only human. It broke my heart and I just wanted to go home straight away and hug my own children so tight. To tell them that I'd always be there for them. We told control that we needed to clean and restock the truck which we did at the hospital while we had a cuppa. Sometimes picking each other up is just hard to do. We cleaned up quietly, both busy in our own minds. When we finished I looked at Colin, 'You OK bud?' I said.

'Always, how about you?' he lied.

I took a deep breath, held back the tears and answered. 'Couldn't be better! Time for a crackhead now then?'

55

'Maybe they'll send us back for a ninety-nine – break – ,' he said with a sarcastic laugh.

We both smiled at each other. The smiles of men who refused to give in to what we were really feeling and I leant forward to push the button that would show control we were clear again for another job. Almost instantly it started beeping to signify there was another job waiting for us. We exchanged a knowing look and then drove back off into the rain. The world may have stopped for those parents and their poor little one. But for the rest of the night-time crews, life went on. Although a bit sadder than before.

I'd like to offer up another bit of a public service announcement at this point. Going out drinking is all well and good. But when you are walking home please take your hands out of your pockets. You see, when you are proper full on rip roaring, dancing in the street, singing songs of unrequited love at the top of your voice whilst telling your best mate that 'I fuckin love you I do' drunk, it's really difficult to get your hands out of your pocket. That was according to our next patient anyway. One minute he was singing his heart out with the love of his life 'We've only known each other for a while ya know but we are just totally best friends' best mate. And the next he was falling nose first towards the floor at a rapid rate of knots. And at least ten miles an hour quicker than he could release his hands from his tight jeans pockets.

The good news was he hadn't cut his hands in any way at all! The bad news that his nose was now spread across most of his face and a couple of his teeth had made a dash for freedom across the pavement. Luckily he was drunk enough not to be in

56

too much pain. This was probably a very different story in the morning.

Another wintry Saturday evening with Jolene in Brighton and the box buzzed into life. Jolene leant forward and pushed the button to bring the information into view.

UNCONCIOUS PATIENT IN THE GARDEN OF THE RAILWAY BELL PUB. WE DON'T THINK THIS IS ANYWHERE NEAR THE RIOT.

We looked at each other and I pushed the button on the radio to call up control.

Dispatcher: 306 go ahead.

Me: 306, errmm, riot?

Dispatcher: Oh yes, didn't you know? There's a riot in town, but it's OK, we don't think it's anywhere near where you're going.

Me: Triffic!

So it turned out that, as it was such a cold night, the Brighton and Portsmouth fans had decided to warm each other up by kicking the shit out of each other. There may have been other reasons, I don't know, I wasn't there when it started. So we trundled off towards the Railway Bell pub, which as you would expect was up near Brighton Station. As we turned off of the main Queens Road into the smaller one-way street that is Surrey Street we noticed a lot of vehicles outside the Railway Bell. On closer inspection they appeared to be police vehicles. Police riot vehicles actually. So far from it being nowhere near the riot it was actually where the riot all began, and was still going on quite happily.

We messaged control who told us to stand off while they spoke to the police on scene. When they got back to us they again advised us to stay where we were but not approach the pub. We were sitting about fifty yards away on a straight one-way street. Jolene wasn't keen on the idea of staying but we sat there and started talking and joking about all the things we pictured going on in that pub. At this point two more vans of riot police appeared. They kitted up and walked to the front door of the pub. The first guy opened the door and we could hear the noise from where we were. We also saw some of the ammunition as glasses, chairs and tables all headed towards the door. The copper at the front calmly turned away, walked back to his crew and nodded across to something behind their van.

That's when we saw several dog handlers walking across the road complete with huge hungry looking wolves on leads! I couldn't believe my eyes as they opened the door, let go of the leads and shut the door again before stepping back a few feet. I imagine there was quite a bit of confusion and a large amount of fear inside the pub at that time. So it took about ten seconds before the front door burst open and people started falling over each other to get out of the pub and run off down the street. Several of them who came out seemed to have large German shepherds attached to them. I know it shouldn't have but this gave me the proper giggles and I couldn't stop laughing.

However, once the initial commotion stopped and the teeth had been removed from people's arses the crowds started milling about in the road we were on. They were clearly still a bit narked and looking for trouble to cause. It was at this point that 'Hotel 900' – the police helicopter hovering above us – decided to turn on its spotlight and light us up like a fucking Christmas tree! It was like a scene out of a zombie film when all of a sudden the herd saw a light and looked up as one. At the big shiny yellow bus with blue lights on the top.

They didn't run towards us or anything but there was a definite shuffle as one in our general direction. What I needed to say didn't seem right for a recorded line so I quickly dialled control on my phone.

'Hello, its 306. Can you tell PC Plod to turn that fucking light off!'

'I think they are just making sure you are safe and they can all see you.'

'Oh yes, they can all see us. Turn it off!'

The message was obviously relayed and the light turned off. A hundred football 'fans' looked up as one. Somehow it seemed to do the trick and just like a moth when the light is turned out they all started drifting off in different directions.

We never did find our patient though!

Alone working on a car one evening and was sitting in one of my favourite standby points by the beach, watching the sun going down and the waves lapping against the shore. I'd been left alone for a while and was quite content and had almost forgotten I was at work for a while. Until, that is, there was a sudden loud knocking on my window which scared the life out of me. I turned to see a very angry-looking lady about to bang on my window again. I wondered if maybe she had mistaken me for police – despite the different colour Battenberg and the big ambulance sign down the side of the car it wouldn't be the first time – as I couldn't really think why she would be looking so angry at me and thought maybe she wanted to report something to them.

I wound the window down and was part way through saying can I help you before she started shouting at me.

'What the fuck do you think you are doing just sitting around! I don't pay my taxes for you to sit on your arse watching the beach. You might as well have an ice cream too while you're at it!'

I looked at her face for any signs of humour; surely she must be having a laugh with me. But as I said it she launched into another tirade at me.

'There are probably people dying out there while you just sit here doing nothing. I saw an ambulance with blue lights on earlier! Why aren't you doing that?'

I think I must have looked a bit shell shocked because I certainly felt it. I tried to explain the fact that I had been placed at a 'strategic' standby point, don't ask me how it's strategically decided. I think they roll a dice until it makes up enough numbers for coordinates and then send you there. I tried to explain that this was how it worked, we didn't just sit on base but would be out and about sent to various points throughout the county in order to be already semi mobile and respond to incidents quicker. I tried to explain that I was in a better position to help people than if I was hidden away somewhere and could cover most of the area in a small amount of time from that point. The one time I really wanted my terrafix to start beeping and sending me somewhere and it decided to stay frustratingly quiet.

I did my best impression of a politician for a while, smiling sweetly whilst she carried on talking at me or telling me what I'd done wrong. I tried several times to interject but eventually got bored and let her blow herself out. I was obviously in a good mood as I didn't just tell her to fuck off and wind the window back up! Eventually she ran out of things to say so walked off, turning back to glare at me angrily. It's amazing how we can upset people without even trying sometimes!

So while on the subject I feel I should address the standby subject. When there used to be lots of ambulance bases in all different towns it was easier to leave them on base if there were no calls. Although sometimes if more than one crew was on base they would quite often send one of you out to a strategic standby point. This was to reduce response times and get people to incidents quicker. And maybe also to make sure we didn't get to chat to other crews and risk an outbreak of morale amongst the staff. However nowadays they are getting rid of most of the ambulance stations and merging all the local crews into one localised superstation or make ready centre. However this obviously means that there are no crews in the individual towns to get to people quickly.

Once upon a time it would have been easy to send crews out to different areas on standby to get around this problem. However these days the ambulance crews are so short-staffed and overwhelmed that standby is extremely rare as there is always another job waiting the second you clear up. Unfortunately the vast majority of these are a complete waste of time and things that really don't need an ambulance. People no longer take responsibilities for their own actions and are very quick to dial up the big yellow taxi. People regularly call for broken fingers or hands, twisted ankles, colds, tummy aches and vomiting. And this isn't even a third of the reasons ambulances get called out.

The problem with this is that whilst we are telling you that yes, we understand your sore throat is very nasty and you do in fact have a bit of a hoarse voice we can't be helping anyone having a heart attack or other more serious concerns.

Unfortunately, due to a litigative society and issues in the past, the protocol states that we have to take at least two sets of clinical observations at least fifteen minutes apart. We then have to write up all notes and explain why we didn't feel the need to take the patient to hospital or who we have discharged their care to. Whilst this might seem like an easy break in the day it takes up a lot of time. Especially when there are quite often at least three cars on the driveway and three other adults in the house.

News flash people, going to hospital in an ambulance does not mean you get seen any quicker than if you drive yourself in. In fact if the crew and the nurse are in agreement that you can go to the waiting room and you didn't need an ambulance you may find it takes even longer! I have been at a patient's house in the past for a sprained/ painful wrist and heard a paediatric resus go out on my radio. Please think about the knock-on effects of your actions if calling for an ambulance and if you really do need one at all.

Sorry, got a bit serious again there! I'll try to stop that.

The alert went off while I was sitting in Brighton in the response car. Male hit in the face with an angle grinder. I grimaced as I imagined the mess I was going to find when I arrived on scene and started making progress through the early evening traffic. People always comment on how much fun it must be to speed through the traffic on lights and sirens and how they'd love to do it. And sometimes they are completely right. It can be great fun and a part of the job that most of us definitely love. But it can also be an absolute ball ache spending the whole time guessing which way people are going to move if they move at all. Nine times out of ten we already know from a long way off who has seen and heard us and are watching their actions in the vehicle to see what they are going to do. And on the flip side we can usually tell exactly who has got the radio turned right up and hasn't used their mirror since brushing their teeth before leaving the house. These ones usually don't realise until we are right up behind them, changing siren tones every five seconds to gather their attention. This is when they swerve at the last minute with no indication and in any random direction that their sudden panic takes them in.

Anyway, it was getting dark as I pulled up at the address and was met by a man standing outside. It always helps when someone has come outside to meet us, especially when it's getting dark and the house numbers aren't obvious. This bloke was obviously pleased to see us as he stood their grinning like a village idiot. Panic brings out lots of unusual responses from people and relief is obviously the classic one when we arrive. To this guy it seemed to bring him great joy.

I got out of the car and as I leant in to grab my bag I said over my shoulder, 'Where's the patient mate?' and was met with the response, 'I'm right here!'
I quickly swung back round thinking the patient must have come out too now which is when I first took a proper look at the grinner. Ah, OK. He wasn't grinning! The angle grinder had obviously bounced back off of the wall and hit him beneath his

nose. What I initially took as a grin was where his top lip had fallen down after the cut was made exposing his teeth. He was remarkably calm about it and I was now the one looking like a village idiot. An ambulance crew arrived and we got him in the back of the truck where I popped a needle in his arm and gave him pain relief while my colleagues dressed his wound. He was then taken off to hospital while I sat there for a few minutes chuckling to myself for thinking he was grinning at me. Oops!

It was a sunny Sunday morning in Hove and we could hear the church bells ringing as we sat down with a bacon sandwich and a cup of tea. Which of course made the alarms go off! Resus in Hove, elderly male. We went downstairs and jumped in the truck. Control called us up en route to say they had no spare vehicle to assign as yet – for a resus it's protocol to try and send more than one vehicle due to it being quite a labour intensive job – and could we let them know if one was still required. Basically if the patient was cold and dead could we let them know as we would then just be sorting out the paperwork and helping the family rather than needing another crew as fast as possible to help out.

We pulled up in the quiet little cul-de-sac and jumped out, grabbing our kit and heading towards the house. A little old lady looking, understandably, very distressed met us at the door.

'Help me,' she said. 'He's in the living room and he's not breathing!'

I took a few large strides up the hallway into the living room whilst my crewmate tried to get a brief history of the incident and looked around. Nothing! It seemed unlikely but I even looked behind the sofa which wasn't completely against the wall. I turned around and looked at the old lady who was walking up the hallway with my crewmate.

'Errm, did you say in here?' I said sounding clearly confused as my crewmate entered and looked around expectantly.

'Oh,' she said. 'He was there a minute ago!'

Guessing that the patient wasn't as ill as she had previously thought I said I would take a look around and went from room to room in hunt of the patient. With a very confused look on my face I came back into the living room shaking my head at my colleague. It was at this point that the doorbell went, so seeing as the immediate emergency didn't seem to be quite what we had believed, I went to answer it. At the door was the next-door neighbour who had been worried on seeing the ambulance and came to check she was OK. I asked her about the lady's husband and she proceeded to tell me that he passed away earlier in the year and the lady was having a hard time accepting it.

This was so sad as the poor lady just hadn't been able to come to terms with the loss of her husband and had at times seen him as he was that day on the floor and struggling, needing our help. Either that or she had called us out for a ghost!

Jobs like this, whilst not needing our medical skills, really put a lot of life and death into perspective. We see the things that we go out to and we do our best to help. But we don't see the long-term effect these things have on the people left behind. It's truly heart breaking sometimes and again shows why we need good people with us and around us. As I've said, a good crewmate is worth their weight in gold. But it also helps having a good partner at home. Someone you can unload to and talk about these situations whether they are funny, sad or sometimes horrific. As can be expected the amount of ambulance staff with a level of PTSD is through the roof due to the continued human sadness or trauma that we witness. And without a decent outlet for what we've been through it would, and in some cases does, eat away at us. The suicide rate in the emergency services is scarily high and I myself have lost some good friends to it in recent years. We all talk about it being OK to not be OK and make sure you talk to someone. But sometimes we are the worst people at taking our own advice.

I'm lucky that my wife is interested in what I do. She knows I sometimes need to vent and she knows when something has affected me. She knows I carry certain ghosts with me. Patients from jobs past that I can see without even having to close my eyes. As real as you are right now reading this book. At least I hope someone's reading this book. There are certain addresses that we drive past and she knows I'm going to say it every time. I just can't help myself. 'Did a resus/ job in there.' She knows I'm going to say it and she never stops me. Because she knows that it was bad enough that in some way it affected me and has stayed with me.

Anyway, I know what you guys are really waiting for. A baby story! Everyone always asks – right after asking what's the worst thing you've ever seen – have you ever delivered a baby. Well yes, yes I have, quite a few in fact. And you know what? I bloody hate them! I don't mean I hate babies, I'm not that bad! It's just that it's a job that can potentially go so wrong for either patient and it's just such a nice feeling when it's done and everyone is still alive and well with lots of smiles and happy tears. Sometimes the patients cry too!

The alert went off and we headed out to the vehicle. As soon as I got in and saw the words Labour/ Childbirth my heart sank. I knew that most of the time we didn't end up delivering and were little more than a big yellow maternataxi but there was the odd occasion. We got there as quick as we could to find mum outside waving her arms around like a windmill. It actually turned out to be mother-in-law and father-in-law and husband were inside where the baby was apparently being born right now. I grabbed a maternity pack and walked into the hallway. It was a long hallway and I walked along until I could see clearly into the living room where the action was taking place.

Sitting on the window sill, texting on his phone was dad – the baby's dad – whilst standing two feet behind the patient who was naked and on all fours was the stepdad doing his best impression of Martin Scorsese directing her to push whilst filming EVERYTHING on his camcorder. I took this view in immediately on entering the room and noticed the one thing missing. There was nobody in place to catch the baby who was literally about to fall out head first onto the carpet. I didn't really have time to think or do anything else, I took three steps and dived onto the floor with my gloved hands out in front of me, just catching the baby as she dropped into my hands! It was a catch worthy of an England goalkeeper and I nearly bounced it twice on the floor before kicking it to the far corner. Then I remembered it was a baby and I'm not a goalkeeper. This had all happened within seconds of us arriving and my crewmate was still getting a brief history of what was going on and how the pregnancy had been. Which means that I was still laying on the floor with my hands under the mother and holding a baby when she walked in a few seconds later.

The end of another shift and we drive back wearily to base. Usually late as we very rarely clear up before being already past our finish time at the hospital. It's not unusual these days to do over two hundred miles in a shift and end up in a different county to your base station. We get back to base and park our vehicle up in a space so that it can be made ready again for the next crew that will use it. We take all of our personal items off, our work iPads, stethoscopes, kit bags, drugs bags and first response bags, personal issue controlled drugs and we cart everything into the building. Everything has to be put into the correct places and signed for. Controlled drugs back into a locked container using biometrics to recognise us. It's been a long day and we're feeling knackered.

As we start to make our way out of the station we see the crews coming in to start their shifts. They ask how it's been and usually aren't too optimistic about the answers. But they laugh and catch up with their shift partners as they get their kit ready and check out their own drugs ready for what's ahead. I say goodbye to my crewmate and tell him to drive safely, I'll see him next week if we don't decide to catch up for a drink in the week.

As I get into my car and put my head back against the headrest, I watch the big metal gates slide open. I see the blues light up on one of the ambulances and the sirens start up as it heads out into the night. Another life to be born, rescued or brought back from the brink!

Or maybe it's just someone else with a dildo stuck up their arse!